# OCEAN ANIMALS

## COLORING BOOK

This book belongs to :

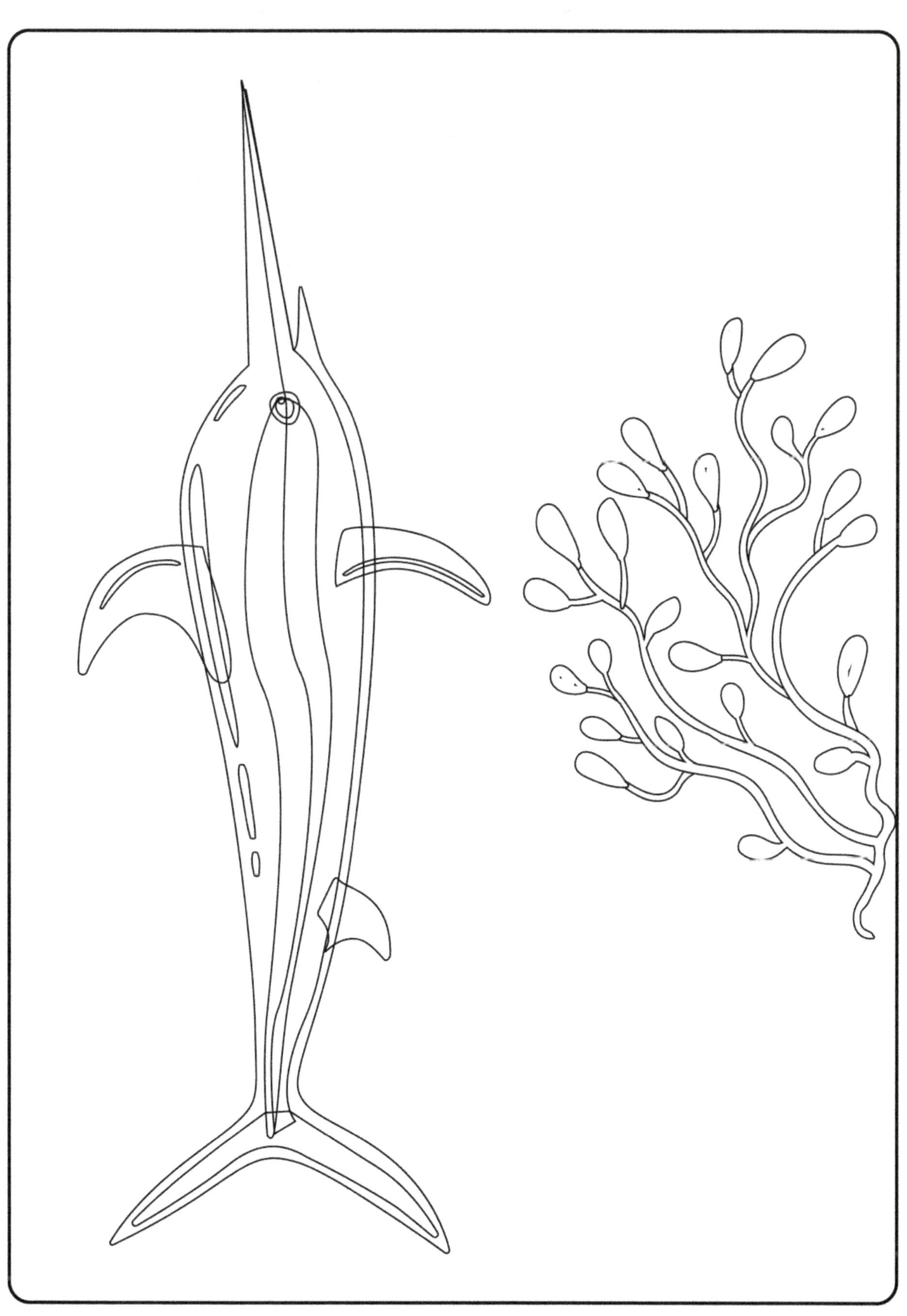

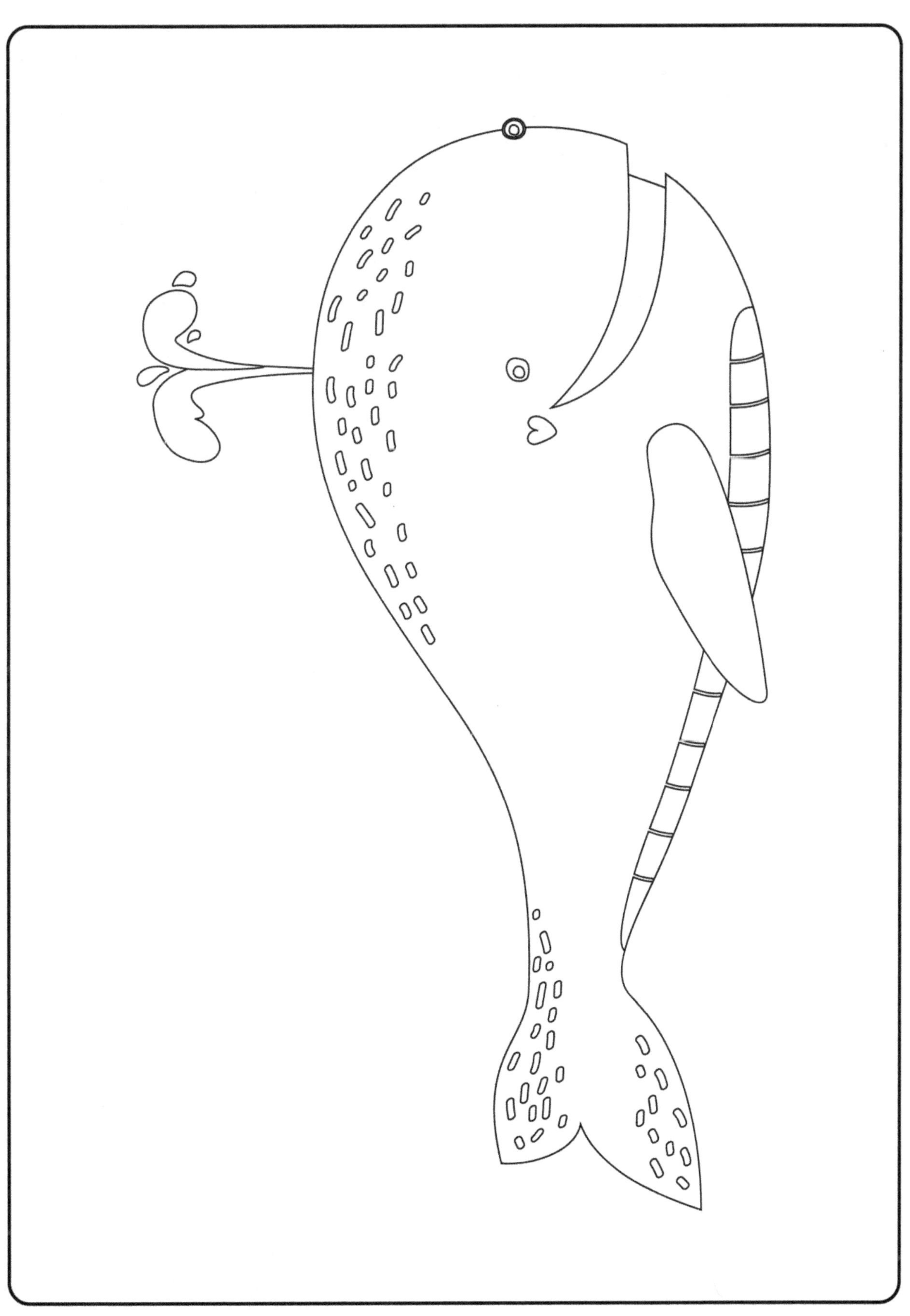

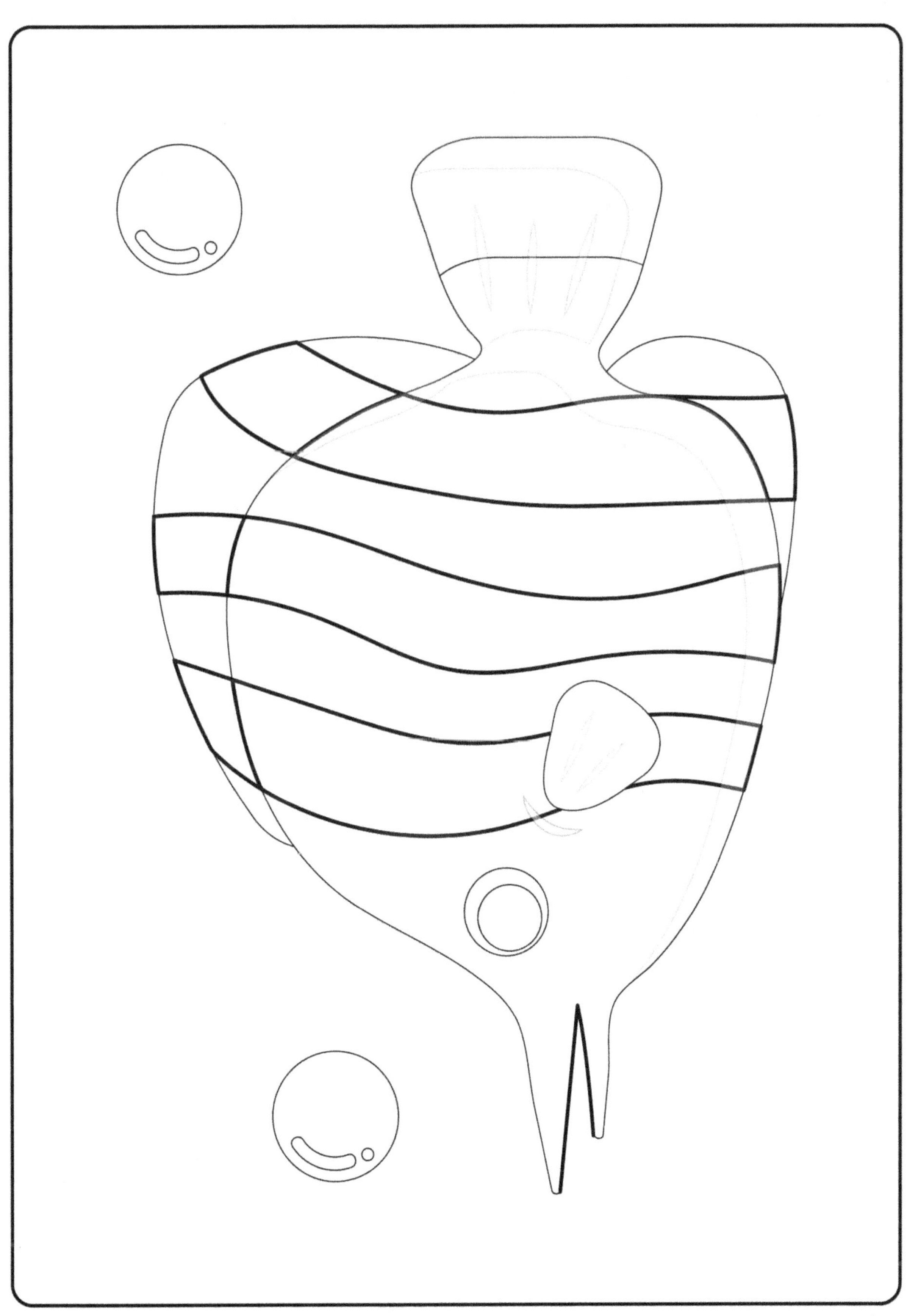

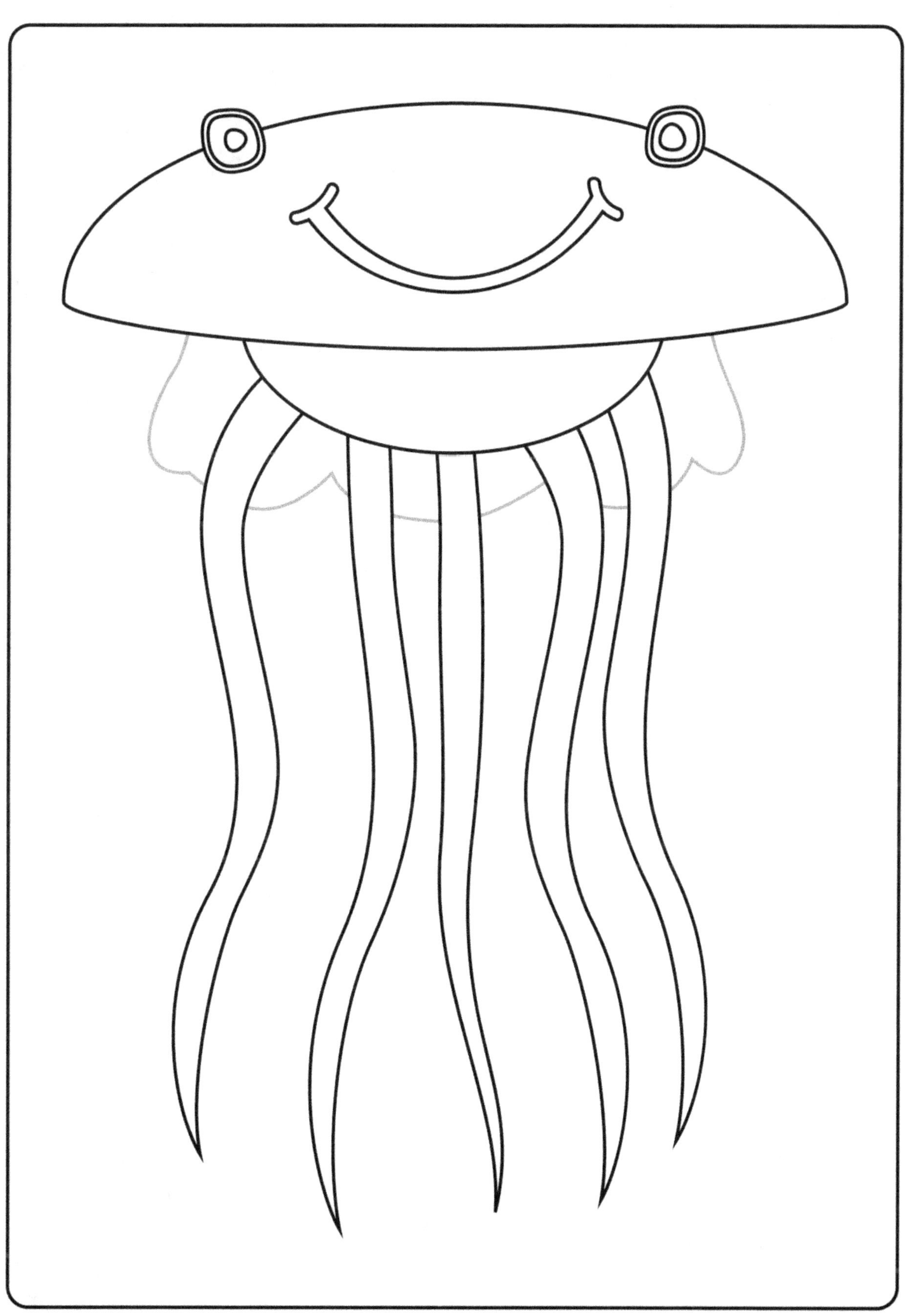

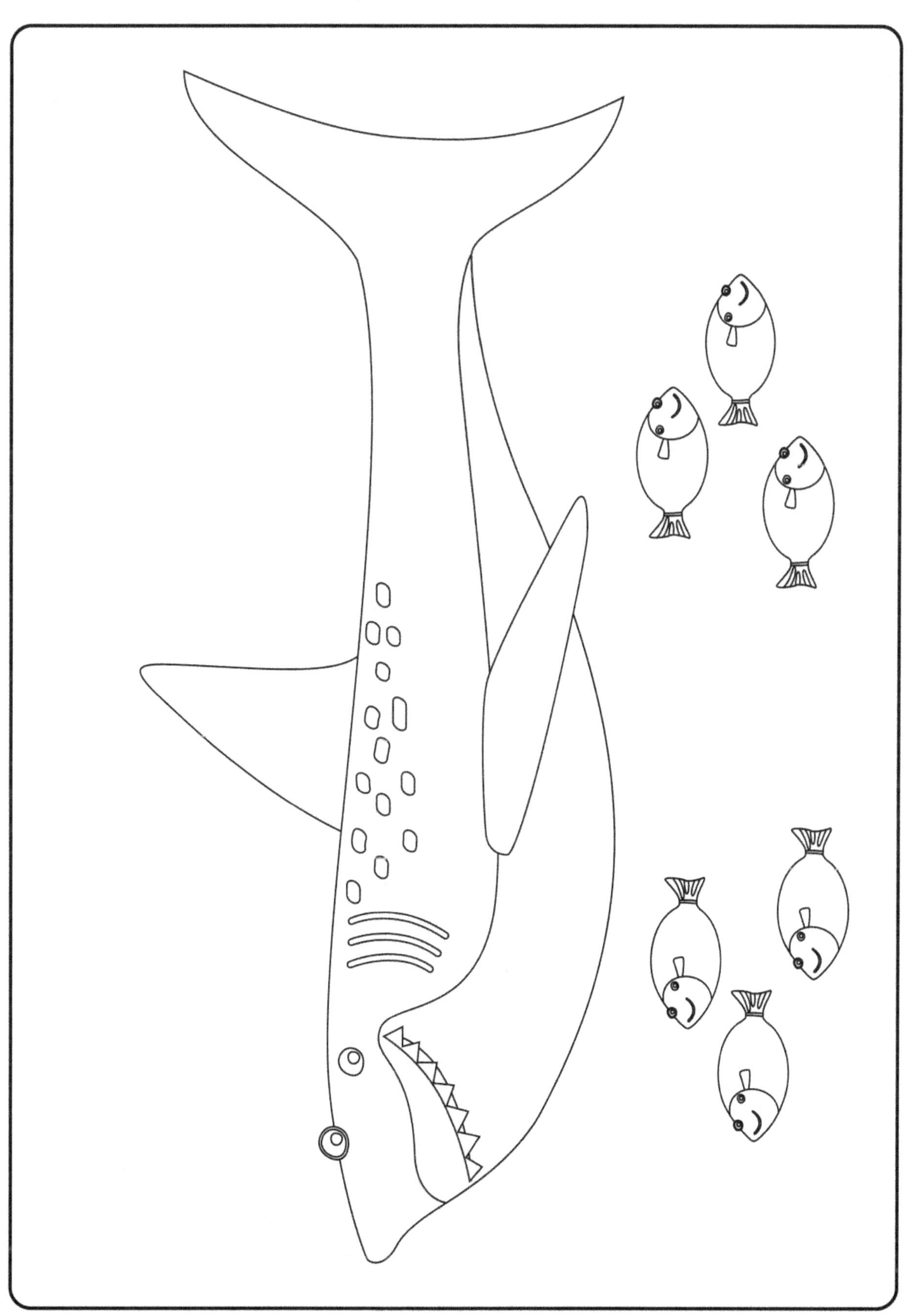

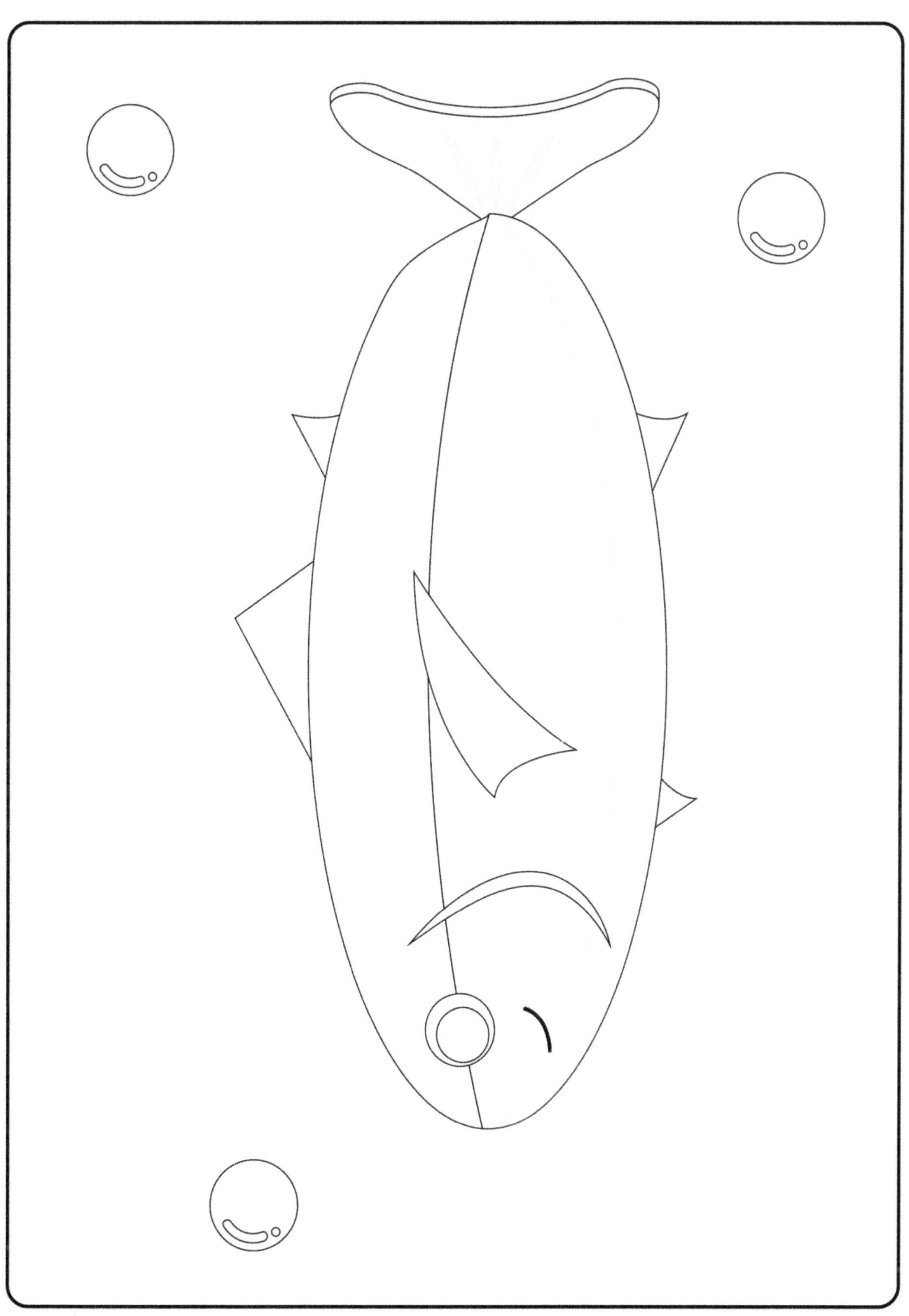

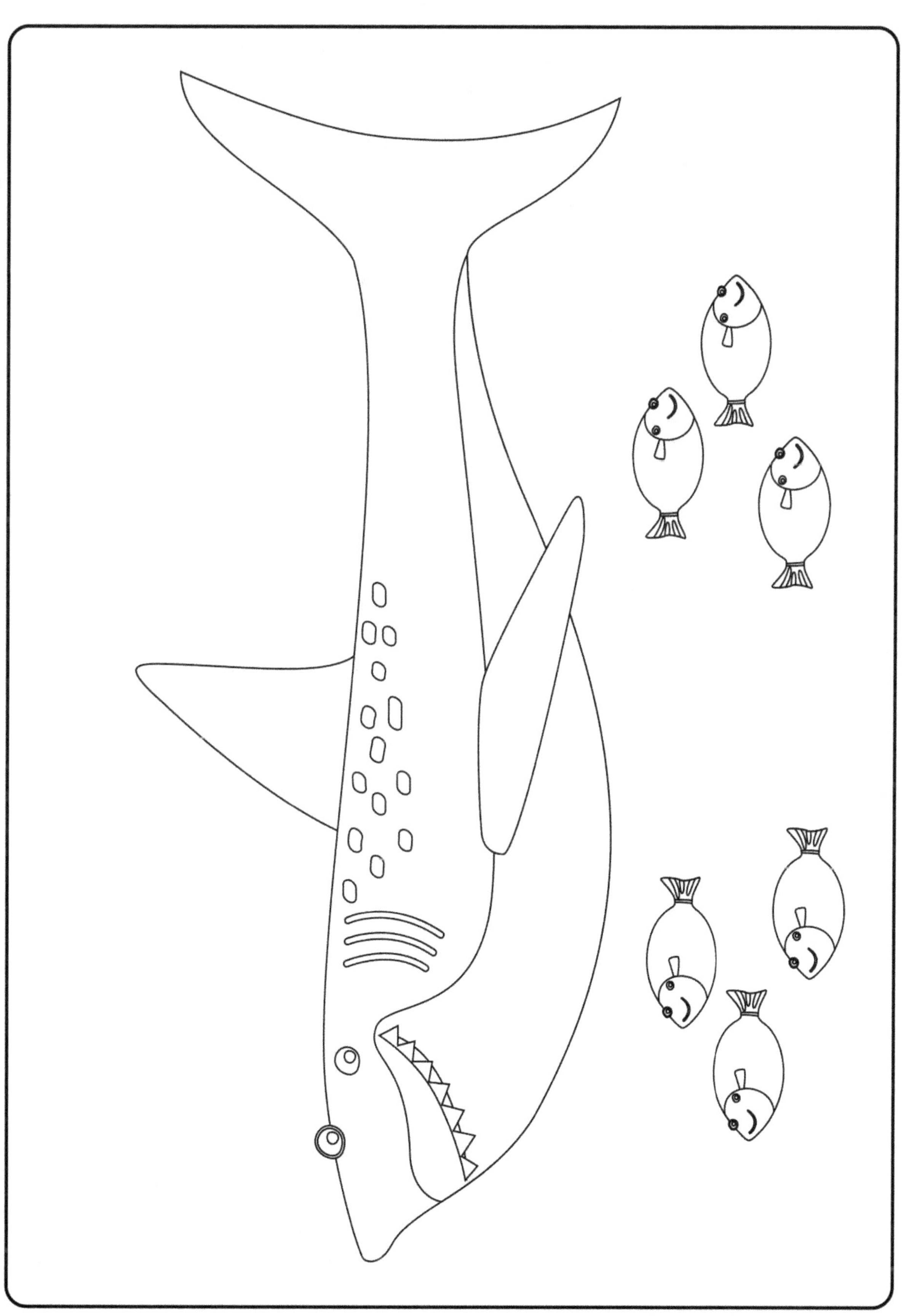

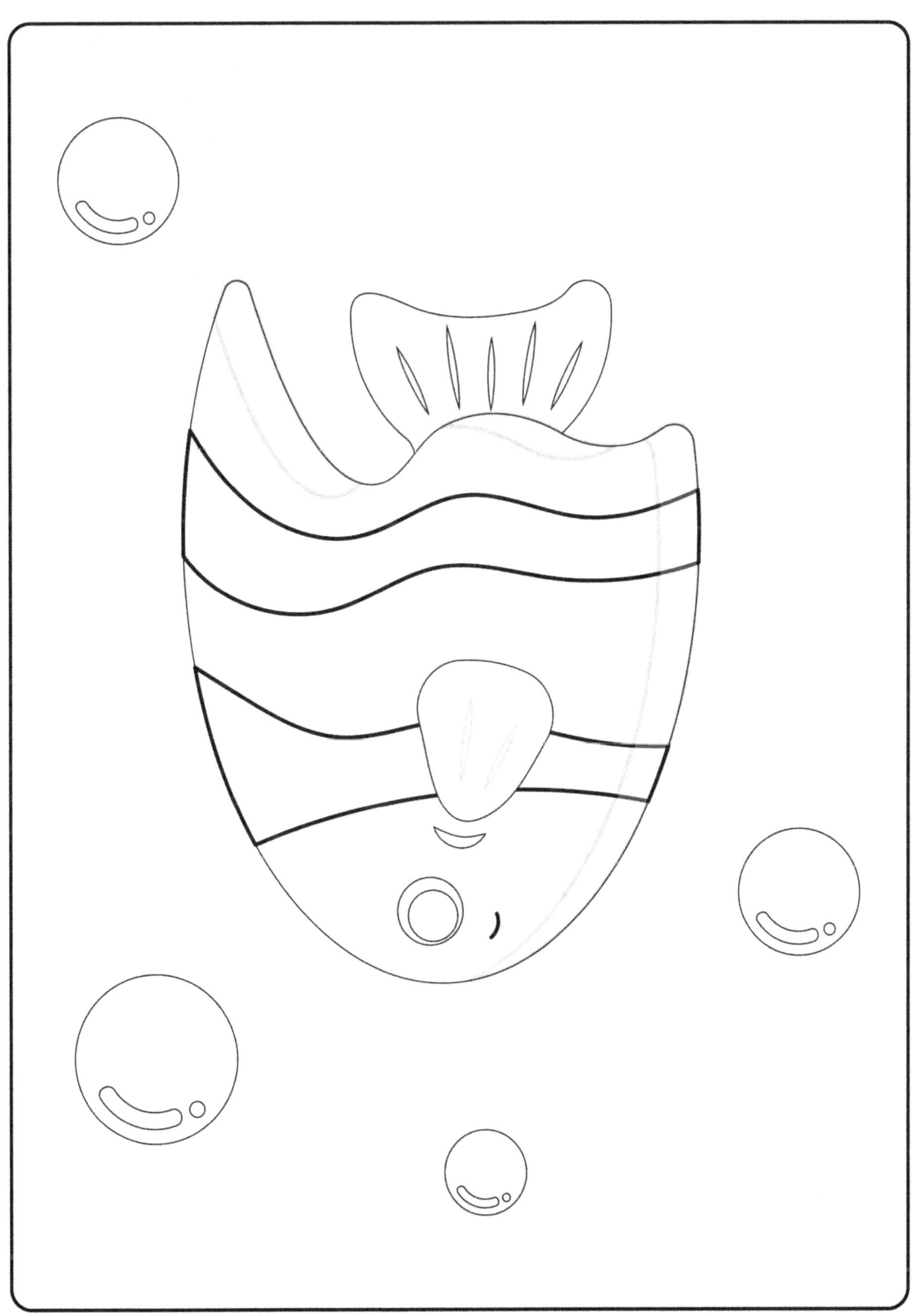

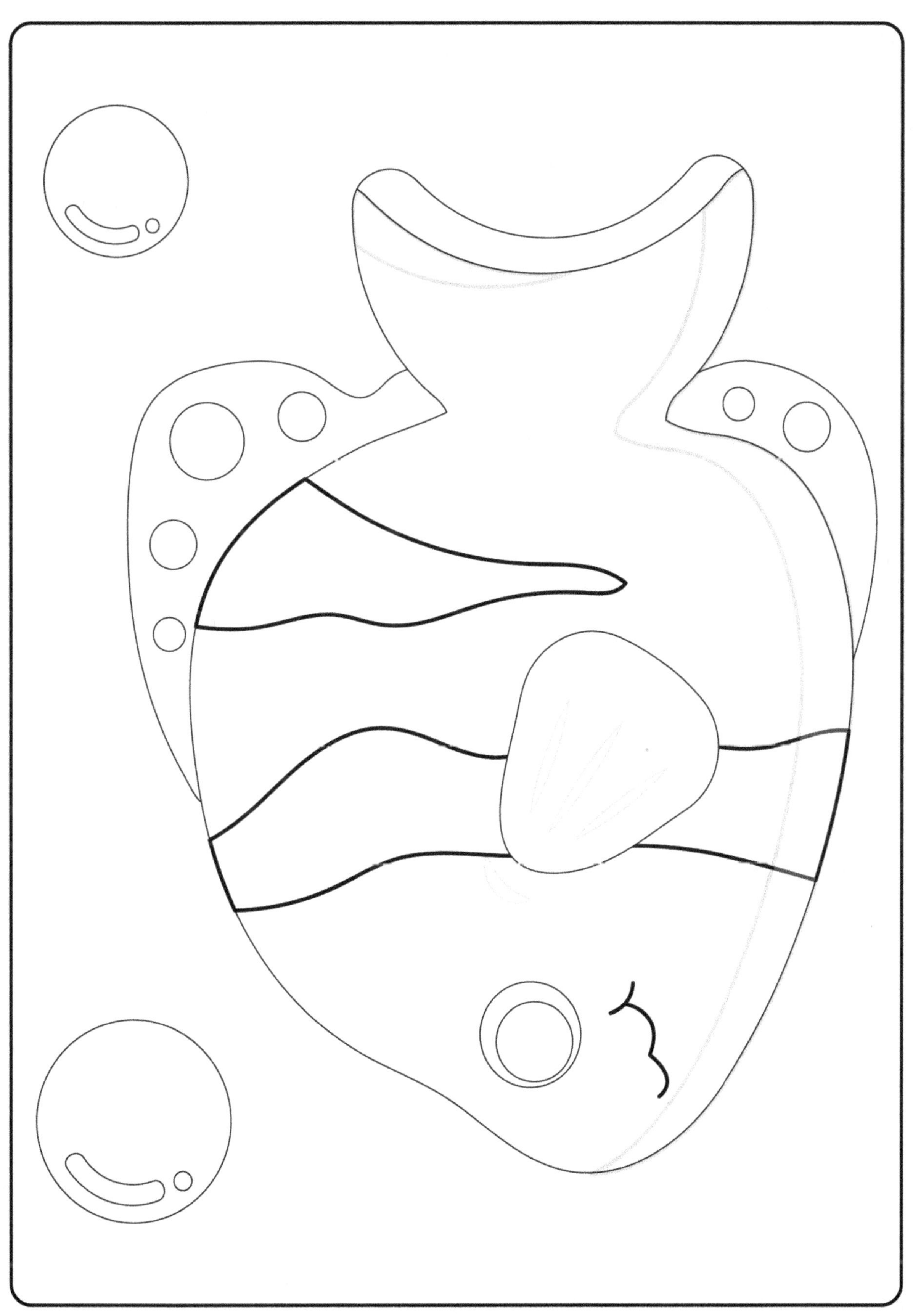

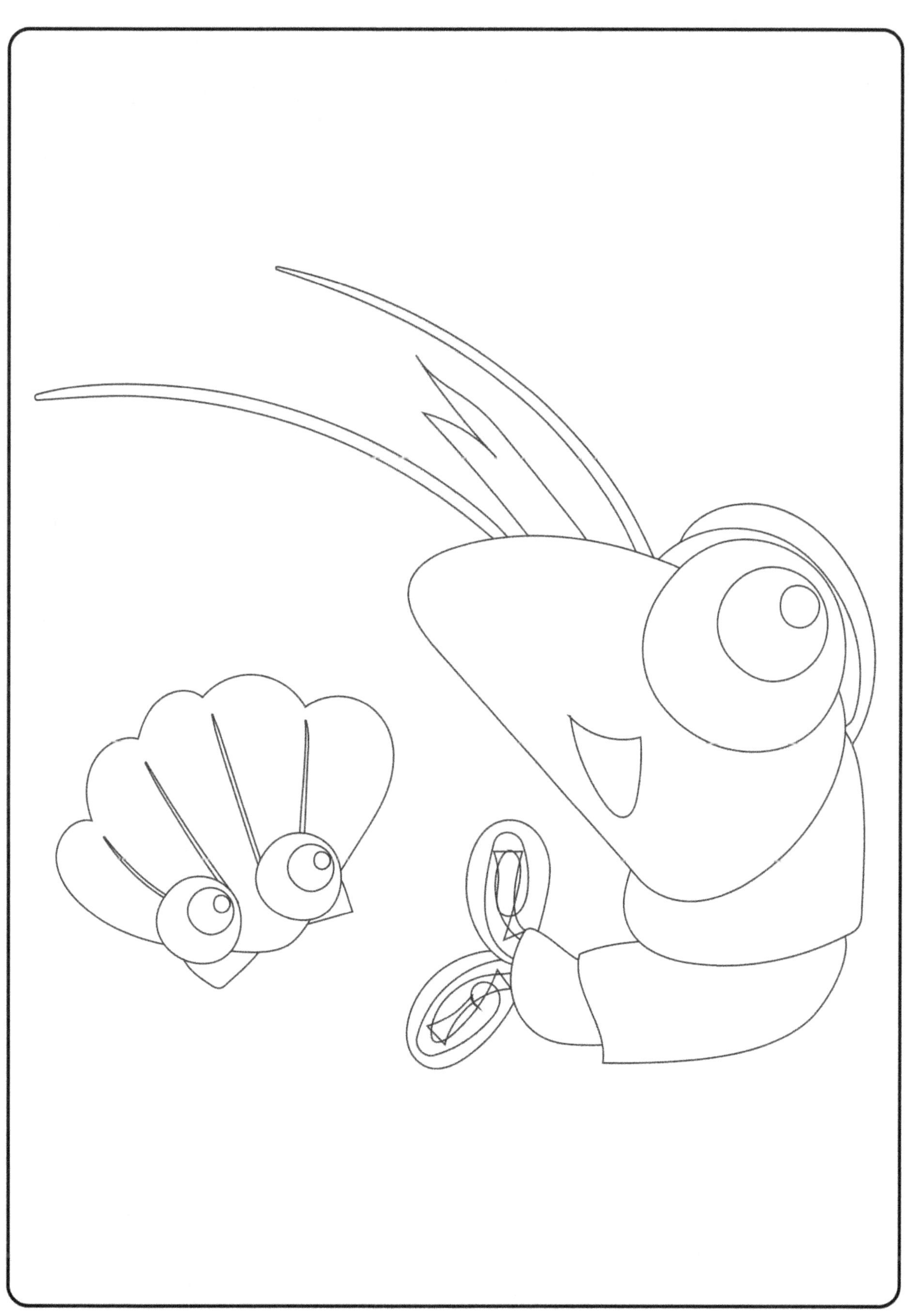

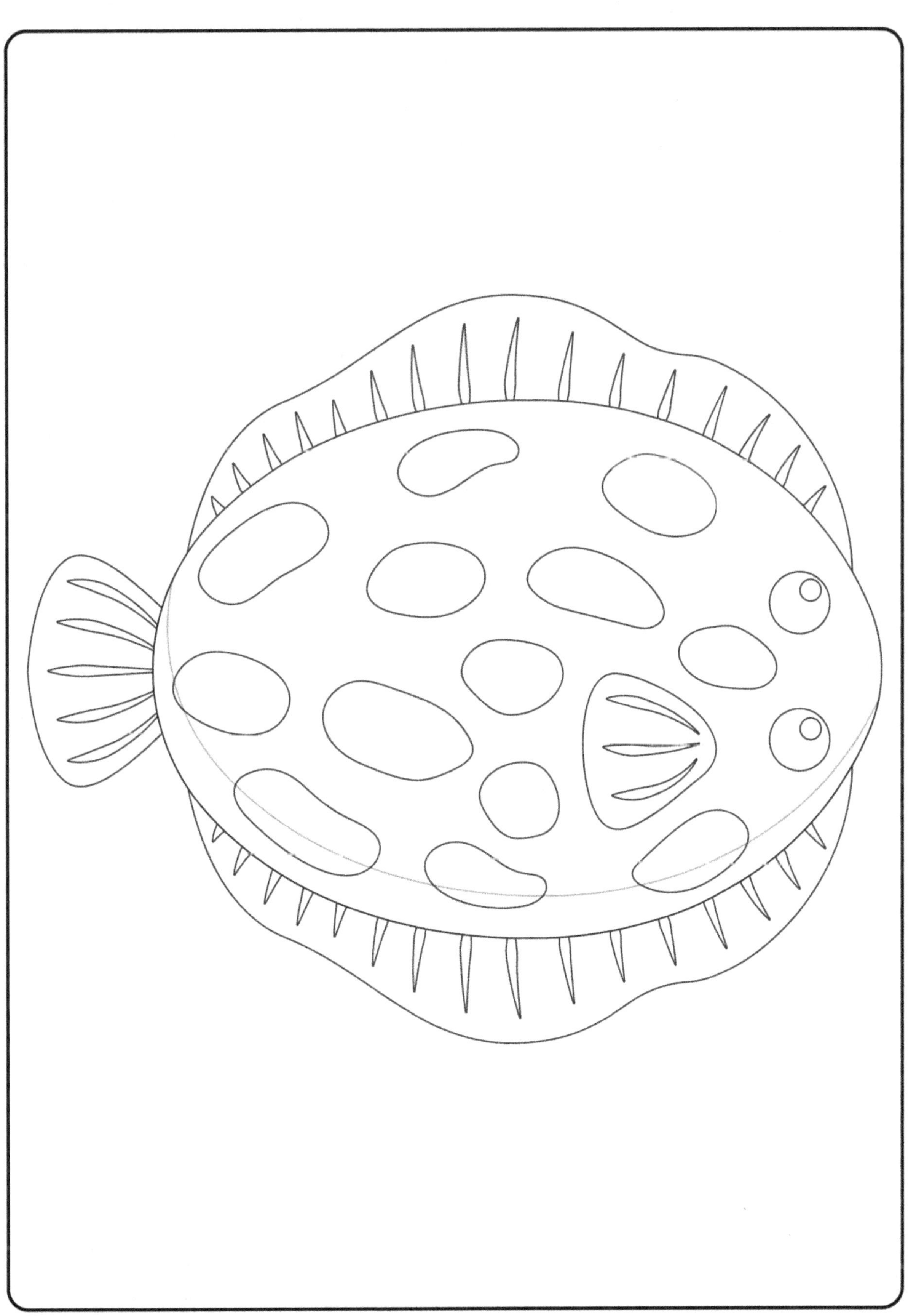